Chinese Graded Reader

Level 1: 300 Characters

秘密花園

Mìmì Huāyuán

The Secret Garden

by Frances Hodgson Burnett

Mind Spark Press LLC

SHANGHAI

Published by Mind Spark Press LLC

Shanghai, China

Mandarin Companion is a trademark of Mind Spark Press LLC.

Copyright © Mind Spark Press LLC, 2013

For information about educational or bulk purchases, please contact Mind Spark Press at business@mandarincompanion.com.

Instructor and learner resources and traditional Chinese editions of the Mandarin Companion series are available at www.MandarinCompanion.com.

First paperback print edition 2013

Library of Congress Cataloging-in-Publication Data
Burnett, Frances Hodgson.

The Secret Garden : Mandarin Companion Graded Readers: Level 1, Simplified Chinese Edition / Frances Hodgson Burnett; [edited by] John Pasden, Yang Renjun, Yu Cui

1st paperback edition.

Shanghai, China / Salt Lake City, UT: Mind Spark Press LLC, 2013

Library of Congress Control Number: 2014943472
ISBN: 9781941875001 (Paperback)
ISBN: 9781941875131 (Paperback/traditional ch)
ISBN: 9780991005208 (ebook)
ISBN: 9780991005253 (ebook/traditional ch)

All rights reserved; no part of this publication may be reproduced, stored in a retrieval system, transmitted in any form, or by any means, electronic, mechanical, photocopying, recording, or otherwise, without the prior written permission of the publishers.

Mandarin Companion Graded Readers

Now you can read books in Chinese that are fun and help accelerate language learning. Every book in the Mandarin Companion series is carefully written to use characters, words, and grammar that a learner is likely to know.

The Mandarin Companion Leveling System has been meticulously developed through an in-depth analysis of textbooks, education programs and natural Chinese language. Every story is written in a simple style that is fun and easy to understand so you improve with each book.

Mandarin Companion Level 1

Level 1 is intended for Chinese learners at an upper-elementary level. Most learners will be able to approach this book after one to two years of formal study, depending on the learner and program. This series is designed to combine simplicity of characters with an easy-to-understand storyline which helps learners to expand their vocabularies and language comprehension abilities. The more they read, the better they will become at reading and grasping the Chinese language.

Level 1 is based on a core set of 300 fundamental characters, ensuring each book's vocabulary will be simple everyday words that the reader is most likely to know. Level 1 books contain approximately 400 unique words, introducing a limited number of new key words relevant to the story.

Key words are added gradually over the course of the story accompanied by a numbered footnote for each instance. Pinyin and an English definition are provided at the bottom of the page for the first instance of each key word, and a complete glossary is provided at the back of the book. All proper nouns have been underlined to help the reader distinguish between names and other words.

What level is right for me?

If you are able to comfortably read this book without looking up lots of words, then this book is likely at your level. It is ideal to have at most only one unknown word or character for every 40-50 words or characters that are read.

Once you are able to read fluidly and quickly without interruption you are ready for the next level. Even if you are able to understand all of the words in the book, we recommend that readers build fluidity and reading speed before moving to higher levels.

How will this help my Chinese?

Reading extensively in a language you are learning is one of the most effective ways to build fluency. However, the key is to read at a high level of comprehension. Reading at the appropriate level in Chinese will increase your speed of character recognition, help you to acquire vocabulary faster, teach you to naturally learn grammar, and train your brain to think in Chinese. It also makes learning Chinese more fun and enjoyable. You will experience the sense of accomplishment and confidence that only comes from reading entire books in Chinese.

Extensive Reading

After years of studying Chinese, many people ask, "why can't I become fluent in Chinese?" Fluency can only happen when the language enters our "comfort zone." This comfort comes after significant exposure to and experience with the language. The more times you meet a word, phrase, or grammar point the more readily it will enter your comfort zone.

In the world of language research, experts agree that learners can acquire new vocabulary through reading only if the overall text can be understood. Decades of research indicate that if we know approximately 98% of the words in a book, we can comfortably "pick up" the 2% that is unfamiliar. Reading at this 98% comprehension level is referred to as "extensive reading."

Research in extensive reading has shown that it accelerates vocabulary learning and helps the learner to naturally understand grammar. Perhaps most importantly, it trains the brain to automatically recognize familiar language, thereby freeing up mental energy to focus on meaning and ideas. As they build reading speed and fluency, learners will move from reading "word by word" to processing "chunks of language." A defining feature is that it's less painful than the "intensive reading" commonly used in textbooks. In fact, extensive reading can be downright fun.

Graded Readers

Graded readers are the best books for learners to "extensively" read. Research has taught us that learners need to "encounter" a word 10-30 times before truly learning it, and often many more times for particularly complicated or abstract words. Graded readers are appropriate for learners because the language is controlled and simplified, as opposed to the language in native texts, which is inevitably difficult and often demotivating. Reading extensively with graded readers allows learners to bring together all of the language they have studied and absorb how the words naturally work together.

To become fluent, learners must not only understand the meaning of a word, but also understand its nuances, how to use it in conversation, how to pair it with other words, where it fits into natural word order, and how it is used in grammar structures. No textbook could ever be written to teach all of this explicitly. When used properly, a textbook introduces the language and provides the basic meanings, while graded readers consolidate, strengthen, and deepen understanding.

Without graded readers, learners would have to study dictionaries, textbooks, sample dialogs, and simple conversations until they have randomly encountered enough Chinese for it to enter their comfort zones. With proper use of graded readers, learners can tackle this issue and develop greater fluency now, at their current levels, instead of waiting until some period in the distant future. With a stronger foundation and greater confidence at their current levels, learners are encouraged and motivated to continue their Chinese studies to even greater heights. Plus, they'll quickly learn that reading Chinese is fun!

About Mandarin Companion

Mandarin Companion was started by Jared Turner and John Pasden who met one fateful day on a bus in Shanghai when the only remaining seat left them sitting next to each other. A year later, Jared had greatly improved his Chinese using extensive reading but was frustrated at the lack of suitable reading materials. He approached John with the prospect of creating their own series. Having worked in Chinese education for nearly a decade, John was intrigued with the idea and thus began the Mandarin Companion series.

John majored in Japanese in college, but started learning Mandarin and later moved to China where his learning accelerated. After developing language proficiency, he was admitted into an all-Chinese masters program in applied linguistics at East China Normal University in Shanghai. Throughout his learning process, John developed an open mind to different learning styles and a tendency to challenge conventional wisdom in the field of teaching Chinese. He has since worked at ChinesePod as academic director and host, and opened his own consultancy, AllSet Learning, in Shanghai to help individuals acquire Chinese language proficiency. He lives in Shanghai with his wife and children.

After graduate school and with no Chinese language skills, Jared decided to move to China with his young family in search of career opportunities. Later while working on an investment project, Jared learned about extensive reading and decided that if it was as effective as it claimed to be, it could help him learn Chinese. In three months, he read 10 Chinese graded readers and his language ability quickly improved from speaking words and phrases to a conversational level. Jared has an MBA from Purdue University and a bachelor in Economics from the University of Utah. He lives in Shanghai with his wife and children.

Credits

Original Author: Frances Hodgson Burnett

Editor-in-Chief: John Pasden

Content Editor: Yu Cui

Adapted by: Yang Renjun

Illustrator: Hu Shen

Producer: Jared Turner

Acknowledgments

We are grateful to Yang Renjun, Yu Cui, Song Shen and the entire team at AllSet Learning for working on this project and contributing the perfect mix of talent to produce this series.

Thank you to Mark Neville who tested it with students in his Chinese class and offered valuable insights and edits. We're grateful to Dong Hua for her academic feedback, and to our enthusiastic testers Erick Garcia, Ben Slye, Brandon Sanchez, and Mary Ann Abejuro.

Thank you to Heather Turner for being the inspiration behind the entire series, and to Song Shen for supporting us and handling all the small thankless tasks.

Special thanks are due Rob Waring, to whom we refer to as the "godfather of extensive reading," for his encouragement, expert advice, and support with this project. Moreover, we will be forever grateful for Yuehua Liu and Chengzhi Chu for pioneering the first graded readers in Chinese and to whom we owe a debt of gratitude for their years of tireless work to bring these type of materials to the Chinese learning community.

Table of Contents

- i   Story Adaptation Notes
- ii   Characters
- v   Locations
- 1   **Chapter 1** 沒有人喜歡的女孩
- 7   **Chapter 2** 去南京
- 13   **Chapter 3** 這個阿姨不一樣
- 21   **Chapter 4** 有人在哭
- 29   **Chapter 5** 秘密花園
- 36   **Chapter 6** 兩個人的秘密
- 42   **Chapter 7** 是他在哭！
- 49   **Chapter 8** 三個人的秘密
- 55   **Chapter 9** 一起去花園
- 60   **Chapter 10** "你可以做到！"
- 65   **Chapter 11** "在花園裡！"
- 70   **Chapter 12** 沒有秘密了
- 75   Key Words
- 80   Appendix A: Character Comparison Reference
- 83   Appendix B: Grammar Points
- 88   Other Stories from Mandarin Companion

Story Adaptation Notes

This story is an adaptation of British author Frances Hodgson Burnett's 1911 classic novel, *The Secret Garden*. This Mandarin Companion graded reader has been adapted into a fully localized Chinese version of the original story. The characters have been given authentic Chinese names as opposed to transliterations of English names, which sound foreign in Chinese. The locations have been adapted to well-known places in China.

The original story begins in India and later moves to Yorkshire, England when Mary Lennox becomes an orphan. In this adaptation, the locations have been adapted to Hainan and Nanjing, China.

Character Adaptations

The following is a list of the characters from *The Secret Garden* in Chinese followed by their corresponding English names from Burnett's original story. There are, of course, other characters in the story besides these, but many do not have exact correspondences to the original. The names below aren't translations; they're new Chinese names used for the Chinese versions of the original characters. Think of them as all-new characters in a Chinese story.

李葉 (Lǐ Yè) - Mary Lennox

馬阿姨 (Mǎ Āyí) - Mrs. Medlock

文先生 (Wén Xiānsheng) - Archibald Craven

文太太 (Wén Tàitai) - Mistress Craven

王樂心 (Wáng Lèxīn) - Martha Sowerby

林爺爺 (Lín Yéye) - Ben Weatherstaff

王樂天 (Wáng Lètiān) - Dickon Sowerby

文思遠 (Wén Sīyuǎn) - Colin Craven

Cast of Characters

李葉
(Lǐ Yè)

馬阿姨
(Mǎ Āyí)

文先生
(Wén Xiānsheng)

文太太
(Wén Tàitai)

王樂心
(Wáng Lèxīn)

林爺爺
(Lín Yéye)

王樂天
(Wáng Lètiān)

文思遠
(Wén Sīyuǎn)

Locations

海南 (Hǎinán)

The southernmost province of China, Hainan is a large tropical island off the southern coast of mainland China. Today it is known as a popular tourist destination for its clear water and white sandy beaches.

南京 (Nánjīng)

A prominent place in Chinese history and culture, Najing has long been one of China's most important cities. Located in east-central China, it is recognized as one of the Four Great Ancient Capitals of China and today is one of China's largest cities and commercial centers.

Chapter 1
沒有人喜歡的女孩

她叫李葉，是一個不太好看的女孩。

李葉出生在海南。海南在中國的最南邊，很遠很遠。李葉的爸爸經常在外面，很少在家。李葉的媽媽是個很好看的女人，她有很多朋友，每天都和朋友一起玩¹。李葉的爸爸媽媽都很忙，他們沒有時間理²他們的女兒。還有，李葉的媽媽好像³一點也不喜歡李葉，她覺得李葉一點也不像她。李葉出生以後，她就告訴家裡的阿姨⁴："如果你們想讓我開心⁵，就不要讓我看到這個孩子。"所以，李葉很少能見到她

---

1 玩 (wán) *v.* to play
2 理 (lǐ) *v.* to pay attention to
3 好像 (hǎoxiàng) *v.* it seems
4 阿姨 (āyí) *n.* maid, housekeeper
5 開心 (kāixīn) *adj.* happy

的爸爸媽媽。

李葉真的跟她的媽媽不一樣,她

看起來又瘦又小，還經常生病。她總是喜歡生氣，生氣的時候總是哭。如果李葉的媽媽聽到她哭，就會很生氣。所有的人都不喜歡這個孩子，他們從來沒有見過這樣的孩子。為了不讓李葉哭，她的阿姨總是很聽李葉的話。李葉喜歡什麼，她的阿姨就給她什麼。李葉覺得在這個家裡只有她的阿姨關心她。

李葉還不到十歲的時候，有一天，她早上起來以後看到一個新的阿姨，又生氣了，因為她想要以前的阿姨。阿姨告訴李葉："她不會來了。"李葉更生氣了，她讓這個新阿姨馬上出去，讓以前的阿姨馬

6 看起來 (kànqǐlai) *vc.* to look (a certain way)
7 瘦 (shòu) *adj.* thin
8 生病 (shēngbìng) *v.* to get sick
9 總是 (zǒngshì) *adv.* always
10 生氣 (shēngqì) *vo.* to get angry
11 哭 (kū) *v.* to cry
12 為了 (wèile) *conj.* for the purpose of, in order to
13 關心 (guānxīn) *v.* to be concerned about

上來。可是很長時間,她的新阿姨沒有回來,她以前的阿姨也沒來。

那一天和平時不一樣,沒有人跟她說話,也沒有人跟她玩。她很不開心,不知道為什麼今天只有她一個人。一定出事了!

14 平時 (píngshí) *tn.* usual; usually
15 一定 (yīdìng) *adv.* definitely
16 出事 (chūshì) *vo.* to have an accident

後來，她聽到媽媽和別人說話，才知道真的出事了。她家裡很多人都生病了，不到兩天就死了很多人。李葉很難過，因為所有人都不理她。她一個人回到房間哭了一會兒，然後睡了很久。她起來的時候，還是沒有人來看她。

"這兒有個孩子！"後來，幾個人發現了又瘦又小的李葉，她一個人在房間裡。

"孩子，你是誰？為什麼在這裡？"有個人問她。

"我叫李葉，我睡了很久。為什麼我的阿姨不來？"李葉問。

"孩子，他們都死了。"

後來李葉才知道，她的爸爸媽媽和以

---

17 後來 (hòulái) *tn.* afterwards
18 難過 (nánguò) *adj.* to feel upset
19 發現 (fāxiàn) *v.* to discover

前的阿姨都死了，別人都走了。沒有人想到這個孩子，因為他們不喜歡她，所以沒有人關心她。

Chapter 2
去南京

李葉的爸爸媽媽死了以後,她在海南沒有別的家人了,但是她有一個叔叔在南京。

他的叔叔是一個很有錢的人。知道李葉的事以後,叔叔讓家裡的阿姨帶李葉來南京。

叔叔家的阿姨姓馬,是一個又高又瘦的女人。李葉很不喜歡她,也不理她。

馬阿姨好像也不喜歡李葉。她覺得孩子應該可愛聽話,但是李葉又瘦又黃,

---

20 家人 (jiārén) *n.* family
21 叔叔 (shūshu) *n.* uncle, father's younger brother
22 帶 (dài) *v.* to bring
23 應該 (yīnggāi) *aux.* should, ought to
24 聽話 (tīnghuà) *vo.* to obey, lit. "to listen to (someone's) words"

總是不理別人，她從來沒有見過這麼不可愛的孩子。

但是馬阿姨很喜歡說話，看到李葉不理她，她就問："你認識你的叔叔嗎？"

"不認識。"李葉說。

"你的爸爸媽媽沒有跟你說過他嗎？"馬阿姨又問。

"沒有。"想到爸爸媽媽很少跟她說話，李葉更不開心了。

"你知不知道你要去一個很奇怪的地方？"馬阿姨問。李葉不說話。馬阿姨覺得這個孩子真奇怪，一點也不關心她要去哪兒。

看見李葉不說話，馬阿姨又說："文先生的

25 奇怪 (qíguài) *adj.* weird, strange

房子很老,已經六百年了。房子裡有一百個房間,房間裡面的東西都很貴。但是很多房間都關著,我們都不可以進去。房子外面有幾個很大的花園,有很多樹。"

李葉覺得叔叔的家很有意思,跟海南很

26 裡面 (lǐmiàn) *n.* inside　　27 有意思 (yǒuyìsi) *adj.* interesting

不一樣。但是她不想讓馬阿姨知道她的想法，所以還是不說話。

"你覺得怎麼樣？"馬阿姨問。

"我沒有想法。"李葉說。

"你跟文先生一樣奇怪。我不知道你為什麼要去南京，但是我知道文先生一定不會跟你說話，因為他從來不關心別人。文先生的身體有病，認識他的太太以前，他從來沒有開心過。"馬阿姨說。

李葉沒想到這個奇怪的叔叔有太太，馬阿姨覺得李葉很想聽，又說："他的太太是一個很好看的女人，文先生很愛他的太太，她死的時候……"

"什麼？她死了？"李葉覺得很奇怪，馬

28 想法 (xiǎngfǎ) *n.* thinking, idea

上問。

"對。太太死了以後,文先生又像以前一樣奇怪了。他在家的時候,總是在房間裡,不想見人,只有很少的人可以看到他。你也別想看到他,你只能自己玩。"馬阿姨說。

李葉坐在車上,想了很久:叔叔家有很大的花園,花園裡有很多樹,很多花;還有一百個房間,但是不可以進去;叔叔是一個奇怪的人……她在南京會怎麼樣,她也不知道。

Chapter 3
這個阿姨不一樣

兩天以後,李葉和馬阿姨到了叔叔家。

李葉覺得這是一個很奇怪的地方。叔叔的房子很大,有很多房間,但是為什麼很多房間的門都關著?外面有很大的花園和草地,但是為什麼看不到人?李葉很不喜歡這個地方。想到以後要住在這裡,她有點生氣,又想哭了。

馬阿姨帶李葉走了很久,最後,她們走進了一個又大又黑的房間。馬阿姨對李葉說:"我們到了。這就是你的房間。文先生現在不想見你,如果他想見你,我

---
29 草地 (cǎodì) *n.* lawn, grassy area

會來告訴你。記住，你只可以在這個房間裡玩，不可以去別的房間。"然後，馬阿姨走了。

很快，天黑了。李葉一個人在這個又大又黑的房間裡，覺得很難過。她哭了一會兒，然後就睡了。

第二天早上，李葉看到一個新的阿姨在房間裡。她不想理這個阿姨，但是新阿姨對李葉說："你好。我叫王樂心。你喜歡這裡嗎？"

"不喜歡。很不喜歡。"李葉說。

"那是因為你剛來這裡。如果你住久一點，你就會喜歡這裡。"王樂心說，"我很喜歡這裡。你看，那邊有一塊大草地，有很

30 記住 (jizhu) *v.* to remember, to memorize

多花,很多樹,還有很多小鳥。天氣好的時候,小鳥會來跟你說話。"

李葉覺得這個阿姨很奇怪,她跟海南的阿姨不一樣。在海南,阿姨從來不跟李葉說很多話。李葉跟她們說話的時候,她們才跟

李葉說話。她們總是很聽李葉的話。李葉讓她們做什麼，她們就做什麼。

李葉看了一下王樂心，她穿著黃衣服，又黑又瘦，但是看起來很健康也很快樂。

"你是我的新阿姨嗎？"李葉問。

"我會幫你做一些事，但是我不會一直在你身邊。"王樂心說。

"那誰給我穿衣服？"李葉問。

"什麼？你不會穿衣服嗎？"王樂心問。

"不會。我從來沒有自己穿過衣服。"李葉說。

"我從來沒有見過你這樣的孩子。你現在應該學會自己穿衣服。"王樂心說。

31 衣服 (yīfu) *n.* clothing
32 健康 (jiànkāng) *adj.* healthy
33 一直 (yīzhí) *adv.* all along
34 學會 (xuéhuì) *vc.* to learn

聽到阿姨這樣對她說話，李葉很生氣，又哭了。她從來沒有見過這樣的阿姨，她不喜歡這個阿姨。

看到李葉哭了，王樂心笑了，說："好了，好了，別哭了。快起來吧，我幫你穿衣服。"她一邊幫李葉穿衣服，一邊對她說自己的家人。："我們家有12個人。爸爸媽媽沒有時間理我們，我們10個孩子就在大草地裡玩。媽媽說外面的好天氣可以讓我們更健康，所以我們家的孩子都像快樂健康的小馬。我的弟弟王樂天今年12歲，他有一隻小馬，又黑又可愛。"

"他在哪裡找到那隻小馬的？"李葉也想有一隻小馬。

"他在大草地裡找到的。那隻小馬是

他的好朋友，每天都跟他一起玩。我弟弟是個好男孩，小鳥和小馬都喜歡他。"王樂心開心地說。

李葉覺得王樂天很有意思。這是她第一次覺得別人有意思。

中午，王樂心給李葉做了很多好吃的東西。但是李葉覺得不餓，不想吃東西。王樂心說："如果我的弟弟妹妹在這裡，他們一定很快就吃完了。他們經常覺得餓，從來沒有吃過這麼多好吃的東西。"

"我從來沒有餓過。所以我不知道什麼是餓。"李葉說。

"今天天氣很好，如果你不想吃東西，就去花園裡玩一會兒吧。"王樂心說。

"誰跟我一起去？"李葉問。

"我沒有時間,你應該自己去。王樂天就是一個人去大草地裡玩的。"王樂心說。聽到王樂天的名字,李葉一下子很想去花園走一走。

王樂心說:"你出門以後,一直往前走,

35 往前 (wǎngqián) *phr.* forward

就可以走到花園。那裡還有一個小花園，十年了，從來沒有人進去過。"

"為什麼？"李葉覺得很奇怪，馬上問。

"十年前，文先生的太太死了。後來他就關了花園，不讓別人進去，他自己也不進去。沒有人知道門在哪裡。我要走了，馬阿姨在叫我。"

Chapter 4
有人在哭

　　王樂心走了以後，李葉一直在想那個小花園。十年了，從來沒有人進過那個花園。它現在是什麼樣子？她很想看一看。叔叔為什麼不讓別人進去？他那麼愛他的太太，為什麼不喜歡他太太的花園？

　　李葉想了很久，最後來到花園裡，想找到王樂心說的那個地方。但是找了很久，她都沒有找到那個小花園。

　　就在李葉想回去的時候，她發現了一隻小鳥。那隻鳥的頭小小的，身體是黑色和黃色的，很可愛。那隻小鳥一邊飛，一

36 樣子 (yàngzi) *n.* appearance

邊快樂地叫,好像在對李葉說:"你好,我們一起玩吧。"

小鳥飛的時候,李葉就在它後面跑。跑到一個果園的時候,李葉看到一個老人。那個老人在種樹。他看起來不怎麼開心,看到李葉以後沒有理她。

"這是什麼地方?"李葉問他。

"一個果園。"老人說。

"那邊是什麼地方?"李葉又問。

"一個菜園。"老人又說。

就在他們說話的時候,那隻小鳥又飛過來了。老人看到小鳥,一下子就笑了。他對小鳥說:"孩子,你飛去哪兒了?我今

37 種 (zhòng) v. to plant (a tree or other plant)

38 不怎麼 (bùzěnme) adv. not very

天一直沒看到你。"

李葉問老人:"你認識這隻鳥嗎?"

老人說:"我們是朋友。它剛出生的時

候，鳥媽媽就死了，它沒有家人。"

李葉聽到老人這樣說，也很難過。她說："我跟它一樣，也是一個人。"

"你就是從海南來的那個女孩嗎？"老人問李葉。

"是的。你叫什麼名字？"李葉問老人。

"我姓林，你叫我林爺爺吧。我在文先生的花園裡做事，已經在這裡40多年了。我也是一個人，沒有別的朋友。"

就在這個時候，小鳥飛走了，飛到了很高的樹上，樹在一面牆後面。李葉問林爺爺："那面牆後面是一個花園嗎？那是我叔叔的太太的花園嗎？我很想進去，可是聽說沒有門。"

39 做事 (zuòshì) *vo.* to do things　　40 牆 (qiáng) *n.* wall

"那個花園十年以前有門，可是現在沒有了。"聽到花園，林爺爺好像不高興了，說："你走吧，我要做事了。"

後來，李葉經常跑去花園，去那兒和小鳥玩。她還想找到那個小花園的門。

有一天吃飯的時候，她一下子吃完了所有的東西。王樂心笑了，對她說："你現在的樣子看起來比以前健康了。以前你又黃又瘦，像黃色的樹葉。我媽媽說得對，外面的好天氣會讓人很健康。"

李葉一直在想那個小花園的事，她問王樂心："我叔叔為什麼不喜歡那個花園？為什麼他關了花園，也不讓別人找到花園的門？"

王樂心說："我知道你一直沒有忘記那個花園。馬阿姨不讓我們說花園的事，所以你記住，我告訴你以後，你一定不要告訴別人。"李葉說："我一定不會告訴別人。"然後王樂心就說："文太太很喜歡那個花園，她和文先生一起打理，從來不讓別人進去。文太太很喜歡坐在花園裡的樹上。有一天，文太太從樹上掉了下來，第二天就死了。文先生很難過，從那以後，他再也沒進去過，也不讓別人進去。我聽說花園在一面很高的牆後面，但是沒有人知道門在哪裡。"

就在這個時候，李葉聽到了一個孩子的哭聲，好像很遠又好像很近。她問

---

41 忘記 (wàngjì) v. to forget
42 打理 (dǎlǐ) v. to take care of
43 掉 (diào) v. to fall
44 聲 (shēng) n. noise, sound

王樂心:"我好像聽到有人在哭!你聽到了嗎?"王樂心一下子很緊張,馬上關了門,說:"我沒有聽到,你一定聽錯了,那是外面的風,沒有人哭。"後來,李葉又聽到了

45 緊張 (jǐnzhāng) *adj.* nervous

關門聲，然後，哭聲就沒有了。王樂心又說："你聽，是風關了門。"但是，看到王樂心緊張的樣子，李葉覺得她沒有說真話。

Chapter 5
秘密花園

第二天上午，天氣很不好，外面的風很大。李葉又想去花園，可是王樂心對她說："你現在很喜歡出去，這很好。可是今天風太大了，有點冷，如果你出去，會生病的。"

李葉問："那我今天做什麼？"

"你為什麼不看書？"王樂心說。

"我沒有書。"李葉說。

"文先生的書房裡有很多書，你可以去那裡看書。但是你要先問問馬阿姨。"王樂心說完就走了。

李葉沒有問王樂心書房在哪裡，也不

想去問馬阿姨，她想自己找到它。李葉想："如果我找不到書房，那也沒關係。我更想知道，別的房間裡有什麼東西。"李葉記得她剛來這裡的時候，馬阿姨就告訴她，叔叔的房子裡有很多房間，但是很多房間都關著，她也不可以去別的房間。所以，她現在很想進幾個房間看看。

那天上午，李葉走了很遠，她想去遠一點的房間看看。她到了一個房間前面，試了一下，打開了門，走了進去。李葉發現那是一個很大的房間，房間裡有很多有意思的東西。後來，李葉打開了更多的房間。她在那些房間裡玩了很久。

中午的時候，李葉餓了，她想回自己

46 記得 (jìde) *v.* to remember　　48 打開 (dǎkāi) *vc.* to open
47 試 (shì) *v.* to try

的房間吃飯。可是，李葉發現她不知道怎麼回去了。她找了很久，還是找不到自己的房間。就在這個時候，她又聽到了那個孩子的哭聲。

"這次的哭聲比昨晚近了一些。"李葉一邊想一邊往哭聲的方向走，她覺得哭聲更近了，好像就在前面的那個房間裡。她想開門，可是，馬阿姨一下子出來了。她看起來很生氣，大聲說："你來這裡做什麼？我告訴過你，你只能在你的房間裡玩。快回去。"

"可是我聽到有人在哭。"李葉說。

"沒有人在哭，你一定聽錯了。快回去，不然我打你。"馬阿姨生氣地帶李葉回

49 方向 (fāngxiàng) *n.* direction   50 不然 (bùrán) *conj.* otherwise

到自己的房間。

　　馬阿姨走了以後，李葉也很生氣。她知道她沒有聽錯，真的有人在哭。

　　下午，外面的天氣好了很多，李葉去

了花園。到了花園裡，李葉覺得開心多了。她看到林爺爺和那隻小鳥也在花園裡。她跑過去，對小鳥說："你還記得我嗎？"

"記得。它怎麼會不記得你？它知道這花園裡所有的事。"林爺爺說。

"如果你記得我，那你能告訴我那面牆裡面是一個花園嗎？"李葉大聲問小鳥。

這時候，小鳥一邊往前飛一邊叫。李葉笑了，也往前跑。跑到一個樹林裡，小鳥飛到樹上，一直對李葉叫，好像在對李葉說話。李葉高興地說："你想讓我上去嗎？"李葉想上去和小鳥玩，可是不小心，她掉了下來。就在這個時候，她發現草地上有一個小東西，很亮，很好看。李葉發現這

51 樹林 (shùlín) *n.* forest
52 小心 (xiǎoxīn) *v.* to be careful
53 亮 (liàng) *adj.* bright

是一個鑰匙,高興地想:"鑰匙!這就是秘密花園的鑰匙嗎?如果是,如果我能找到秘密花園的門,我就可以進去了。可是,門在哪裡?"

李葉對小鳥說:"小鳥,謝謝你幫我找到了鑰匙。你一定知道花園的門在哪裡,快告訴我吧。"就在這個時候,樹林裡有了很大的風,李葉看到牆邊的一些樹一直在

鑰匙 (yàoshi) *n.* key   秘密 (mìmì) *n.* secret

動。她好像看到了一個黑色的東西，她走過去看了一下，高興地說："是門，是秘密花園的門！"

她用鑰匙小心地打開門，走進去，然後關上了門。

這個花園很奇怪，外面是牆，裡面有很多花、草和樹，可是它們好像都死了。"這裡以前一定很好看。"李葉小聲說，"已經十年了，這十年裡，我是第一個進花園的人。"

李葉在花園裡看了很久，發現這裡還有一些綠色的草和葉子，她一下子很開心："這裡的花和草沒有死。我要讓這個花園像以前一樣好看！"

56 關上 (guānshang) *vc.* to close

Chapter 6
兩個人的秘密

天黑以後,李葉才從花園出來。她今天很開心,因為她找到了秘密花園,這是她的秘密。

"我明天還要來。"李葉對自己說。

回到房間以後,李葉很餓,吃了很多東西。她一邊吃飯一邊問王樂心怎麼種花、種草。她問的時候很小心,不想讓王樂心發現她的秘密。

"我想要一些種花的工具。"李葉說。

"你要用這些工具做什麼?"王樂心問她。

工具 (gōngjù) *n.* tool

"我想要一個自己的花園,種一些花、草和樹。"李葉說。

"你說得對,你應該有一個自己的小花園,我覺得它會讓你開心的。"王樂心說,"可是,你沒有地,你應該讓文先生給你一塊地。"

"那你能幫我買那些工具嗎?"李葉問。

"沒問題,我可以讓我弟弟王樂天幫你買。花、草、樹這些事,他什麼都懂。他買了這些工具以後,我讓他送來。"王樂心開心地說。

"真的嗎?我可以見到王樂天了,我一直很想見他。"李葉高興地說。

兩天以後,李葉很早就去了花園,因

問題 (wèntí) *n.* problem

為今天王樂天會在花園等她，給她送種花的工具。

到了花園以後，李葉看到一個男孩，他身邊還有很多小鳥和一隻小馬，他在學小鳥的叫聲。他看到李葉以後，開心地笑了，說："你是李葉吧？我是王樂天。這是你要的種花的工具和種子。"王樂天很瘦，可是很好看。

"對，我是李葉。謝謝你。你為什麼學小鳥的叫聲？"李葉問。

"因為我們是朋友，我剛剛在和它們說話。"王樂天說。

李葉覺得很有意思，王樂天能聽懂小鳥說話，小鳥也能聽懂王樂天說話。"你能

種子 (zhǒngzi) *n.* seed

給我看一下種子嗎?"李葉問。

"好。這些種子的花是黃色的,那些是紅色的。這裡還有一些工具,你可以種花、種草。"然後他又告訴李葉怎麼種花和種草。最後,他對李葉說:"告訴我你的花園在哪裡,我們可以一起種花。"

李葉一下子很不好意思，她不知道要不要告訴他。但是她覺得王樂天是個好人，他能讓秘密花園像以前一樣好看。她覺得應該告訴王樂天自己的秘密。過了一會兒，她說：「我告訴你一個秘密，但是你不可以告訴別人。」

王樂天馬上說：「沒問題。我一定不告訴別人。我從來沒有告訴別人這些小鳥的家在哪裡。」

「我找到了我叔叔的秘密花園，找到了鑰匙，我還找到了花園的門。我想打理那個花園，讓它像以前一樣好看。你能幫我嗎？」李葉小聲說。

「真的嗎？我以前聽說過那個花園，我也很想去。它在哪兒？」王樂天很高興。

"跟我來。"李葉說。然後,她帶王樂天去了那個秘密花園。

王樂天在花園裡看了很久,然後說:"這個地方很好看。但是它好像睡了很久。"他在花園裡走了一會兒,又說:"這裡的花、樹和草沒有都死。你看,這裡還有一些綠色。我們可以讓它像以前一樣好看。"

那天,李葉和王樂天一直在打理秘密花園,天黑了才出來。最後,王樂天說:"以後我每天都會來這裡幫你。"

"你不會告訴別人,是不是?"李葉問。

"放心吧,不會的。這個花園是我們兩個人的秘密。"王樂天笑了,李葉知道他說的是真話。

60 放心 (fàngxīn) v. to relax, to be relieved

Chapter 7
是他在哭！

那天晚上，外面的風聲很大，李葉沒辦法睡覺，她覺得這風聲聽起來像哭聲。一下子，風聲沒有了，李葉真的聽到了哭聲。李葉覺得很奇怪，為什麼總是有哭聲？這哭聲是從哪兒來的？她要再去看一看。

太晚了，所有的人都睡了，外面只有李葉一個人。"上次，我是在一個房間的外面看到馬阿姨的，她那麼生氣，哭聲一定就在那個房間裡。"李葉想。她很快找到了那個房間。"沒錯，真的有人在房間裡哭。"

李葉馬上打開門，走了進去。她發現這

---

61 辦法 (bànfǎ) *n.* way, method　　62 睡覺 (shuìjiào) *vo.* to sleep

個房間很大,裡面的家具很新,有一張大床,上面有一個男孩。"是他在哭!"李葉太緊張了,不知道應該說什麼,只是看著這

63 家具 (jiājù) n. furniture

個男孩。他看起來10歲左右,身體很瘦,一點兒也不健康,好像病了很久。

"你是誰?"男孩不哭了,好像也很緊張。

"你是誰?"李葉也問他。

"我是文思遠。"男孩說。

"我是李葉,文先生是我的叔叔。我的爸爸媽媽都死了,所以我從海南來到這裡。"李葉說。

左右 (zuǒyòu) *adv.* about, more or less, lit. "left-right"

"文先生是我爸爸。"男孩又說。

"叔叔有一個兒子！"李葉覺得很奇怪，"為什麼阿姨和叔叔都沒告訴過我？我也從來沒見過你？"

"我不想讓別人看見我，也不想讓別人說到我。"男孩說。

"為什麼？"李葉問。

"因為我身體不好，總是生病。我快死了。"男孩一下子又哭了。

"這裡真的很奇怪，總是有那麼多秘密。"李葉想。然後她又問男孩："你爸爸常常來看你嗎？"

"不，他很少來。馬阿姨說他又去旅行了。我媽媽在我出生的時候就死了，

65 常常 (chángcháng) *adv.* often　　66 旅行 (lǚxíng) *v.* to travel

他見到我的時候總是想到我媽媽，所以他恨我，不想見到我。"男孩難過地說。

"因為你媽媽死了，所以你爸爸也恨那個秘密花園？"李葉問。

"什麼秘密花園？"男孩問。

"那是你媽媽喜歡的花園。你媽媽死了以後，叔叔就關了花園。十年了，沒有人進去過，也沒有人知道鑰匙和花園的門在哪裡。"李葉說。

"我可以讓阿姨找花園的鑰匙，讓她們帶我去花園。"

李葉一下子很緊張，她覺得自己不應該告訴文思遠秘密花園的事。如果文思遠告訴了別人，她和王樂天就沒有秘密了。所

67 恨 (hèn) v. to hate

以李葉說：" 如果你讓別人帶你去花園，那個花園就不是秘密了。"

" 秘密？什麼意思？" 文思遠問。

" 你想想，如果我們能找到秘密花園，它就是我們自己的花園。我們可以進去玩，沒有人知道我們在哪裡。多有意思，對不對？" 李葉說。

文思遠一下子懂了，他說：" 我從來不知道什麼是秘密，可是我覺得有秘密會很不錯。"

李葉又說：" 我們可以一起去秘密花園，你的病很快就會好的。"

文思遠一下子笑了，高興地說：" 我很想去那個秘密花園。以後你要經常來這裡。如果你不來，我就讓王樂心去找你。"

李葉也笑了，她知道為什麼王樂心聽到哭聲的時候那麼緊張了。李葉說：「好，我明天再來。記住，那個花園是我們的秘密，不要告訴別人。」說完，李葉就回自己的房間了。

Chapter 8
三個人的秘密

第二天天氣很好，李葉很早就起床了，她想先去秘密花園，因為王樂天在那裡等她，他們要一起打理花園。然後，她要去看一看文思遠。

那天，李葉和王樂天在秘密花園裡做了很多事。他們種了很多紅色和黃色的花、綠色的草，還種了很多樹，花園比以前好看了。

從花園出來以後，李葉馬上就去看文思遠了。文思遠給李葉看他的書，李葉告訴文思遠很多海南的事，他們在一起笑，

---

68 起床 (qǐchuáng) *vo.* to get out of bed

很快樂。

文思遠的阿姨覺得很奇怪。這個男孩從來不笑,只會哭,但是他看到李葉以後,快樂了很多。

"我覺得你應該見見王樂天,他跟你太不一樣了。"李葉說。

"王樂天是誰?"文思遠問。

李葉很喜歡說王樂天:"他是王樂心的

弟弟，今年 12 歲。他會和小鳥說話，每天都去大草地，他知道小鳥住在什麼地方。"

"我什麼都沒見過，因為我有病。我不能去大草地，也不能去花園。"文思遠難過地說。

"為什麼不能？可能很快你就可以去。"李葉說。

"不，我不能，我要死了。別人都這麼說。"文思遠說。

"你不會死。只要你每天出門，外面的好天氣就會讓你的身體很健康。"李葉說。

有一天，李葉很晚才從花園回來。王樂心很緊張地說："你知道文思遠的事了，對嗎？他現在很生氣，因為你沒有去

---

69 可能 (kěnéng) *adv.* possibly, maybe

看他。他已經哭了很久了。馬阿姨也不知道應該怎麼辦，你快去看看吧。"

文思遠看到李葉以後，生氣地問："你今天為什麼沒來？"

"因為我和王樂天有很多事要做。"李葉說。

文思遠更生氣了，大聲說："以後我不讓他再去我的花園。"

李葉也生氣了，她也大聲說："如果你不讓他去花園，我就再也不來看你了。"

文思遠又哭了，哭聲很大。馬阿姨和王樂心更緊張了，王樂心對李葉說："請你讓他別哭了。如果他再哭，他又會生病的。"

李葉看看文思遠，他一直睡在床上，每天都在等自己跟他說話，李葉也覺得有

點難過。她走過去,小聲對文思遠說:"別哭了!如果你不哭,我就告訴你秘密花園的事。"聽到秘密花園,文思遠一下子不哭了,馬上問:"你找到鑰匙了?"

李葉說:"對,我找到了花園的門和鑰匙。你現在睡覺吧,我明天和王樂天一起帶你去秘密花園。"文思遠笑了,很快就睡了。

Chapter 9
一起去花園

因為第二天要去秘密花園,所以文思遠很早就起床了。

為了不讓別人知道他們的秘密,文思遠對馬阿姨說:"今天我要去花園裡走走。但是我不想看到別人。我去的時候,所有人都不可以在花園裡。我回來以後,他們才可以進花園。"

馬阿姨聽到文思遠這樣說,覺得很奇怪。因為文思遠很少出門,也不喜歡出門。馬阿姨說:"我以為你不喜歡出門。"

"如果就我一個人,我一定不想出去,但是這次李葉會和我一起去。"文思遠說。

"我跟你們一起去吧?外面有點冷,如果你不小心,你會生病的。"馬阿姨緊張地說。

"我不要你去。跟李葉在一起,我就會好很多。王樂天也會和我們一起去,沒問題。"文思遠說。

聽到王樂天的名字,馬阿姨就放心了。因為知道大草地的人都知道王樂天。大家都覺得王樂天是一個又健康又喜歡幫別人的人。"如果王樂天可以幫你,那我就放心了。他是這裡最好的男孩。"馬阿姨說。

過了一會兒,王樂天和李葉就來了。因為文思遠身體一直不好,總是睡在床上,很少下床走路,所以他很難走到花園。

70 走路 (zǒulù) *vo.* to walk

王樂天找到了一個輪椅,他們要用這個輪椅幫文思遠去花園。

出門以後,文思遠很高興。他坐在輪椅上,一會兒看看天,一會兒看看樹,他從來沒有覺得花園這麼好看。"你聽,是鳥的叫聲嗎?我很久沒出門了,快忘了鳥的叫聲了。"文思遠問李葉。

"是的。是小鳥,它們在跟你說話。今天你能來花園,它們很高興。"李葉高興地說。

因為文思遠不讓別人去花園,所以這個時候,花園裡沒有別人。但是他們不想讓別人發現他們的秘密,所以先在大花園裡玩了一會兒。

---

71 輪椅 (lúnyǐ) *n.* wheelchair

"到了。"李葉又緊張又高興地說,"這就是秘密花園的門。"

"是這裡!快,我要進去。"文思遠高興地大聲說。他們小心地進了花園,然後關了門。

Chapter 10
"你可以做到！"

文思遠坐在輪椅上，認真地看了一下秘密花園，就像李葉和王樂天第一次來這裡的時候一樣。這次，秘密花園好像比以前好看了，很多黃色和紅色的花都開了，綠草也從地下出來了，樹比以前高了。為了這個男孩，花園可能也想讓自己更好看。

"我真不知道應該說些什麼！我快十一歲了，十一年有很多天，但是今天是我最快樂的一天！"文思遠小聲說。

"是的。我覺得這一定是最好的一天。"王樂天說。

認真 (rènzhēn) *adj.* serious, earnest

"那裡還有樹！可是看起來有點奇怪。"文思遠對李葉說。

李葉知道，文思遠的媽媽就是從樹上掉下來的。她不想讓文思遠難過，就說："它很老了。但是幾個月以後，所有的花和葉子就會長出來。到時候，它就是最好看的樹。"

後來，文思遠就坐在輪椅上，看李葉和王樂天打理花園。他又快樂又難過，說："我真喜歡這裡！以後我每天都要來。可是，如果我能像你們一樣，可以走，可以種花、種草就好了。"

"你會的。你馬上就會很健康。你會跟我們一樣，每天走路來花園！"李葉說。

"走路？我行嗎？"文思遠問。

"一定行！"李葉馬上說。

就在這個時候，他們聽到有人很生氣地說："你們怎麼進去的？快出來！"他們往上看，發現林爺爺就在牆外面，很生氣地看著他們。

李葉一下子不知道應該怎麼辦，她緊張地說："林爺爺，是小鳥幫我找到這個花園的。"

這是第一次別人對文思遠這樣說話。他坐在輪椅上，也很生氣。他問林爺爺："你知道我是誰嗎？"

林爺爺認真地看了一下文思遠，好像一下子想到了什麼，說："是你！你跟你媽媽長得一樣！你就是那個小病人！"

"我不是病人！不是！"文思遠更生氣了。

"他不是。"李葉也生氣了，大聲說。

"如果你沒生病，怎麼一直坐在輪椅上？你怎麼不起來？你如果真的沒生病，就走過來。過來！"林爺爺說。

"文思遠，你能做到，你一定能做到。你起來！"李葉說。

"看著我！"文思遠大聲說。他一下子從輪椅上起來了，小心地走，走了很久，最後，他走到了牆邊。文思遠哭了，然後高興地說："你們看，我沒有病，我做到了！"李葉和王樂天也高興地哭了。

Chapter 11
"在花園裡！"

文思遠不想讓別人知道他們的秘密，所以他讓李葉帶林爺爺進了秘密花園。他告訴林爺爺："以前，這裡是我媽媽的花園。現在它是我的花園了，我喜歡這裡。可是這是一個秘密，你不能告訴別人，只有我、李葉、王樂天和你知道。"

林爺爺說："你媽媽很喜歡這個花園，她經常讓我幫她打理。你媽媽死了以後，你爸爸關了這個花園。可是我也不想讓這個花園死。所以，你們放心吧，這也是我的秘密，我不會告訴別人。"

那天下午，從花園回房間以後，文思遠覺

得很餓，他吃了很多東西。馬阿姨覺得有點奇怪，對文思遠說："你今天在外面太久了。你覺得身體怎麼樣？"

"沒問題，我覺得好多了。明天我還要去花園。"文思遠說。

後來，天氣好的時候，文思遠每天都去花園。他每天都在花園裡走一走，看看花、草和樹，和小鳥一起玩。有時候，他還幫李葉和王樂天打理花園。回房間以後，他總是覺得很餓，吃很多東西。

李葉高興地發現，文思遠的身體健康了很多，也很少生氣了。阿姨們看到文思遠跟以前很不一樣，都覺得很奇怪。

有一天，在花園裡，文思遠坐在輪椅上，對李葉和王樂天說："我不會告訴別人我的身體健康多了,這是我最大的秘密。我每天都要坐輪椅來這裡。我爸爸回來以後,我會自己走到他的房間,對他說'我來了。我的身體很健康,是花園幫了我。以後,我要做一個有用的男人!'"

在花園裡,文思遠和李葉都學會了很多。他們學會了不該只想到自己。現在,他們常常想到花園、王樂天和小鳥。他們比以前更可愛了。

就在文思遠的身體一點點好起來的時候,文先生還在北京旅行。他去了很多地方,但是沒有太太,他在每個地方都不開心。

有一天,文先生在一個花園裡睡覺的

---

73 有用 (yǒuyòng) *adj.* useful

時候，好像看到了他的太太。

"你在哪兒？我好想你！"文先生問。

"在花園裡！在花園裡！"文太太一直說。

文先生回到房間以後，有人告訴他家裡出了大事，讓他馬上回家。

Chapter 12
沒有秘密了

幾天以後,文先生回到了南京。剛到家,馬阿姨就跑過來告訴他:"先生,思遠他……"

文先生一下子很緊張,問:"他怎麼了?"

"他和以前不一樣了。"馬阿姨又說。

"他現在在哪裡?"文先生不太緊張了。

"在花園裡。"馬阿姨說。

"在花園裡!"文先生大聲說。

他馬上去了花園。可是他已經十年沒來這裡了,也忘了鑰匙在哪裡。他不知道為什麼太太讓他來這裡。這個時候,他聽到了花園裡孩子的笑聲。

"有人在裡面!"文先生想,"太奇怪了。十年了,沒有人進過這個花園!他們怎麼會有這個花園的鑰匙呢?我要進去看看。"

文先生剛要開門,一個孩子很快地跑了出來。但是看到文先生,這個孩子馬上不跑了。文先生看了看這個男孩子,高高的,瘦瘦的,看起來很健康。

"爸爸!"這個男孩子叫他。

"你是⋯⋯思遠嗎?"文先生問。

"是我,爸爸,我是思遠!你不認識我了嗎?"文思遠從來沒有想過他會跟爸爸這樣見面,但是現在見到爸爸,他還是很高興。他都快哭了。

文先生一下子不知道說什麼，只是小聲說："在花園裡！在花園裡！"

"是的。"文思遠說，"因為這個花園，我好多了。但是阿姨們都不知道我好了，這是個秘密，因為我想讓你第一個知道。"

文先生哭了，他高興地哭了。他對文思遠說："我以為這個花園已經死了！"

"以前李葉也這麼想，"文思遠說，"但是，它現在好了。它跟以前一樣好看了。"

後來，他們進了花園，跟李葉和王樂天一起坐在樹下。文先生告訴了他們很多花園和文太太的事。文先生第一次覺得關了這個花園是錯的；第一次覺得這個花園沒有死；第一次覺得和思遠在一起也可以很快

樂。文先生和思遠一樣，覺得在很長很長的時間裡他們從來沒有這麼快樂過。最後，文思遠說：「這再也不是秘密花園了，我再也不要坐輪椅了。爸爸，我們一起走回去吧。」

馬阿姨和王樂心看到文先生和一個健康快樂的男孩子一起走回來的時候，

她們覺得很奇怪,但是又很高興。因為她們看到了:這個健康快樂的男孩子就是文思遠!

Key Words 關鍵詞 (Guānjiàncí)

1. 玩 (wán) *v.* to play
2. 理 (lǐ) *v.* to pay attention to
3. 好像 (hǎoxiàng) *v.* it seems
4. 阿姨 (āyí) *n.* maid, housekeeper
5. 開心 (kāixīn) *adj.* happy
6. 看起來 (kànqǐlai) *vc.* to look (a certain way)
7. 瘦 (shòu) *adj.* thin
8. 生病 (shēngbìng) *v.* to get sick
9. 總是 (zǒngshì) *adv.* always
10. 生氣 (shēngqì) *vo.* to get angry
11. 哭 (kū) *v.* to cry
12. 為了 (wèile) *conj.* for the purpose of, in order to
13. 關心 (guānxīn) *v.* to be concerned about
14. 平時 (píngshí) *tn.* usual; usually
15. 一定 (yīdìng) *adv.* definitely
16. 出事 (chūshì) *vo.* to have an accident
17. 後來 (hòulái) *tn.* afterwards
18. 難過 (nánguò) *adj.* to feel upset
19. 發現 (fāxiàn) *v.* to discover
20. 家人 (jiārén) *n.* family
21. 叔叔 (shūshu) *n.* uncle, father's younger brother
22. 帶 (dài) *v.* to bring
23. 應該 (yīnggāi) *aux.* should, ought to
24. 聽話 (tīnghuà) *vo.* to obey, lit. "to listen to (someone's) words"
25. 奇怪 (qíguài) *adj.* weird, strange
26. 裡面 (lǐmiàn) *n.* inside
27. 有意思 (yǒuyìsi) *adj.* interesting
28. 想法 (xiǎngfǎ) *n.* thinking, idea
29. 草地 (cǎodì) *n.* lawn, grassy area
30. 記住 (jìzhu) *vc.* to remember, to memorize

31. 衣服 (yīfu) *n.* clothing
32. 健康 (jiànkāng) *adj.* healthy
33. 一直 (yīzhí) *adv.* all along
34. 學會 (xuéhuì) *vc.* to learn
35. 往前 (wǎngqián) *phr.* forward
36. 樣子 (yàngzi) *n.* appearance
37. 種 (zhòng) *v.* to plant (a tree or other plant)
38. 不怎麼 (bùzěnme) *adv.* not very
39. 做事 (zuòshì) *vo.* to do things
40. 牆 (qiáng) *n.* wall
41. 忘記 (wàngjì) *v.* to forget
42. 打理 (dǎlǐ) *v.* to take care of
43. 掉 (diào) *v.* to fall
44. 聲 (shēng) *n.* noise, sound
45. 緊張 (jǐnzhāng) *adj.* nervous
46. 記得 (jìde) *v.* to remember
47. 試 (shì) *v.* to try
48. 打開 (dǎkāi) *vc.* to open
49. 方向 (fāngxiàng) *n.* direction
50. 不然 (bùrán) *conj.* otherwise
51. 樹林 (shùlín) *n.* forest
52. 小心 (xiǎoxīn) *v.* to be careful
53. 亮 (liàng) *adj.* bright
54. 鑰匙 (yàoshi) *n.* key
55. 秘密 (mìmì) *n.* secret
56. 關上 (guānshang) *vc.* to close
57. 工具 (gōngjù) *n.* tool
58. 問題 (wèntí) *n.* problem
59. 種子 (zhǒngzi) *n.* seed
60. 放心 (fàngxīn) *v.* to relax, to be relieved
61. 辦法 (bànfǎ) *n.* way, method
62. 睡覺 (shuìjiào) *vo.* to sleep

63. 家具 (jiājù) *n.* furniture
64. 左右 (zuǒyòu) *adv.* about, more or less, lit. "left-right"
65. 常常 (chángcháng) *adv.* often
66. 旅行 (lǚxíng) *v.* to travel
67. 恨 (hèn) *v.* to hate
68. 起床 (qǐchuáng) *vo.* to get out of bed
69. 可能 (kěnéng) *adv.* possibly, maybe
70. 走路 (zǒulù) *vo.* to walk
71. 輪椅 (lúnyǐ) *n.* wheelchair
72. 認真 (rènzhēn) *adj.* serious, earnest
73. 有用 (yǒuyòng) *adj.* useful

Part of Speech Key

adj. Adjective

adv. Adverb

aux. Auxiliary Verb

conj. Conjunction

cov. Coverb

mw. Measure word

n. Noun

on. Onomatopoeia

part. Particle

prep. Preposition

pn. Proper noun

tn. Time Noun

v. Verb

vc. Verb plus complement

vo. Verb plus object

Discussion Questions
討論問題 (Tǎolùn Wèntí)

Chapter 1 沒有人喜歡的女孩

1. 李葉是一個什麼樣的女孩？為什麼沒有人喜歡李葉？
2. 你知道海南嗎？海南是什麼樣的地方？
3. 李葉的媽媽好像一點也不喜歡李葉。你覺得真的有這樣的媽媽嗎？

Chapter 2 去南京

1. 你知道南京嗎？你覺得南京怎麼樣？
2. 你喜歡文先生這樣的家嗎？為什麼？
3. 你覺得文太太死了以後，文先生有什麼變化 (biànhuà)？

Chapter 3 這個阿姨不一樣

1. 王樂心跟李葉以前的阿姨有什麼不一樣？
2. 你覺得王樂心的家和李葉的家有什麼不一樣？
3. 如果王樂心和李葉經常在一起，你覺得她們會有什麼變化 (biànhuà)？
4. 你有王樂心這樣的朋友嗎？說一說他們是什麼樣的人。

Chapter 4 有人在哭

1. 林爺爺是一個老人，你覺得他可以做李葉的朋友嗎？
2. 如果你是李葉，你會用什麼辦法進秘密花園？
3. 為什麼文太太死了以後，文先生關了秘密花園？

Chapter 5 秘密花園

1. 你覺得是誰在哭？為什麼？
2. 如果你是李葉，馬阿姨總是生氣，你會聽她的話嗎？
3. 想象一下，李葉走進秘密花園以後，看到了一個什麼樣的花園？

Chapter 6 兩個人的秘密

1. 李葉為什麼很喜歡王樂天？王樂天是什麼樣的人？
2. 李葉為什麼會告訴王樂天她找到了秘密花園的鑰匙？
3. 如果你是李葉，你會告訴王樂天花園的秘密嗎？為什麼？

Chapter 7 是他在哭！

1. 你會和文思遠這樣的人做朋友嗎？為什麼？
2. 文先生為什麼很少去看文思遠？
3. 你覺得李葉應該讓文思遠知道秘密花園的事嗎？為什麼？

Chapter 8 三個人的秘密

1. 認識李葉以後，文思遠有了什麼變化 (biànhuà)？
2. 如果你是李葉，看到文思遠那麼生氣，你會怎麼做？

Chapter 9 一起去花園

1. 文思遠是怎麼不讓別人知道他們的秘密的？
2. 你覺得秘密花園會讓文思遠發生什麼變化？

Chapter 10 "你可以做到！"

1. 現在的花園有了什麼變化？
2. 如果你是林爺爺，看到三個孩子在秘密花園裡，你會怎麼做？
3. 文思遠為什麼要站起來？

Chapter 11 "在花園裡！"

1. 文思遠為什麼不讓別人發現他比以前健康了？
2. 秘密花園讓文思遠和李葉學會了什麼？

Chapter 12 沒有秘密了

1. 如果你是文思遠，看到文先生的時候，你會說什麼？
2. 文先生看到現在的秘密花園以後，他的想法有什麼變化？

Appendix A:
Character Comparison Reference

This appendix is designed to help Chinese teachers and learners use the Mandarin Companion graded readers as a companion to the most popular university textbooks and the HSK word lists.

The tables below compare the characters and vocabulary used in other study materials with those found in this Mandarin Companion graded reader. The tables below will display the exact characters and vocabulary used in this book and not covered by these sources. A learner who has studied these textbooks will likely find it easier to read this graded reader by focusing on these characters and words.

Integrated Chinese Level 1, Part 1-2 (3rd Ed.)

Words and characters in this story not covered by these textbooks:

Character	Pinyin	Word(s)	Pinyin
葉	yè	李葉 葉子	Lǐ Yè yèzi
密	mì	秘密	mìmì
秘	mì	秘密	mìmì
鳥	niǎo	鳥	niǎo
聲	shēng	聲	shēng
門	mén	門	mén
樹	shù	樹	shù
草	cǎo	草	cǎo
奇	qí	奇怪	qíguài
怪	guài	奇怪	qíguài
林	lín	林	lín
鑰	yào	鑰匙	yàoshi
匙	shi	鑰匙	yàoshi
總	zǒng	總	zǒng

Character	Pinyin	Word(s)	Pinyin
輪	lún	輪椅	lúnyǐ
風	fēng	風	fēng
牆	qiáng	牆	qiáng
掉	diào	掉	diào
恨	hèn	恨	hèn
向	xiàng	向	xiàng

New Practical Chinese Reader, Books 1-2 (1st Ed.)

Words and characters in this story not covered by these textbooks:

Character	Pinyin	Word(s)	Pinyin
葉	yè	李葉 葉子	Lǐ Yè yèzi
姨	yí	阿姨	āyí
密	mì	秘密	mìmì
秘	mì	秘密	mìmì
叔	shū	叔叔	shūshu
鳥	niǎo	鳥	niǎo
草	cǎo	草	cǎo
奇	qí	奇怪	qíguài
怪	guài	奇怪	qíguài
健	jiàn	健康	jiànkāng
康	kāng	健康	jiànkāng
直	zhí	一直	yīzhí
緊	jǐn	緊張	jǐnzhāng
輪	lún	輪椅	lúnyǐ
椅	yǐ	輪椅	lúnyǐ
更	gèng	更	gèng
黃	huáng	黃色	huángsè

Character	Pinyin	Word(s)	Pinyin
牆	qiáng	牆	qiáng
具	jù	工具	gōngjù
近	jìn	近	jìn
恨	hèn	恨	hèn

Hanyu Shuiping Kaoshi (HSK) Levels 1-3

Words and characters in this story not covered by these levels:

Character	Pinyin	Word(s)	Pinyin
葉	yè	李葉 葉子	Lǐ Yè yèzi
王	wáng	王	Wáng
密	mì	秘密	mìmì
秘	mì	秘密	mìmì
知	zhī	知道	zhīdao
從	cóng	從	cóng
像	xiàng	像	xiàng
死	sǐ	死	sǐ
林	lín	林	Lín
緊	jǐn	緊張	jǐnzhāng
輪	lún	輪椅	lúnyǐ
更	gèng	更	gèng
海	hǎi	海	hǎi
牆	qiáng	牆	qiáng
具	jù	工具	gōngjù
往	wǎng	往	wǎng
掉	diào	掉	diào
恨	hèn	恨	hèn

Appendix B: Grammar Point Index

For learners new to reading Chinese, an understanding of grammar points can be extremely helpful for learners and teachers. The following is a list of the most challenging grammar points used in this graded reader.

These grammar points correspond to the Common European Framework of Reference for Languages (CEFR) level A2 or above. The full list with explanations and examples of each grammar point can be found on the Chinese Grammar Wiki, the definitive source of information on Chinese grammar online.

CHAPTER 1	
Modifying nouns with phrase + "de"	[Phrase] + 的 + Noun
Measure words for counting	Number + Measure Word + Noun
"Not very" with "bu tai"	不太 + Adj.
Modifying nouns with adjective + "de"	Adj. + 的 + Noun
"Zai" following verbs	Verb + 在 + Place
The "zui" superlative	最 + Adj.
Pronoun "mei" for "every"	每 + Measure Word (+ Noun)
Expressing "every" with "mei" and "dou"	每 + Measure Word + Noun + 都 + Adj./Verb
Expressing "and" with "he"	Noun 1 + 和 + Noun 2
Expressing "together" with "yiqi"	一起 + Verb
The "all" adverb	都 + Verb/ 都 + Adj.
Expressing "in addition" with "haiyou"	Clause 1，還有 + (,)+ Clause 2
"It seems" with "haoxiang"	好像……
"Not at all"	一點(兒)也不……
"If…, then…" with "ruguo…, jiu…"	如果……，就……
Causative verbs	Noun 1 + 讓/叫/請 + Noun 2……

Result complements "dao" and "jian"	Verb+ 到 / 見
Measure words to differentiate	這 / 那 + Measure Word (+ Noun)
Expressing ability or possibility	能 + Verb
"Both A and B" with "you"	又……又……
Expressing "and also" with "hai"	還 + Verb
"Always" with "zongshi"	總是 + Verb
At the time when	……的時候
Auxiliary verb "hui" for "will"	會 + Verb
Special verbs with "hen"	很 + Verb
Referring to "all" using "suoyou"	所有……都……
"Never" with "conglai"	從來不/從來沒 (有)
Expressing experiences with "guo"	Verb + 過
Comparing specifically with "xiang"	Noun 1 + 像 + Noun 2 + (那麼……)
Explaining results with "suoyi"	……,所以……
Expressing purpose with "weile"	為了 + Purpose + Verb
Expressing "as one likes" with "jiu"	還 + Verb/ Adj.
Continuation with "hai"	還 + Verb/ Adj.
Again in the past with "you"	又 + Verb
Explaining causes with "yinwei"	Result,因為 + Reason
"Would like to" with "xiang"	想 + Verb
Wanting to do something with "yao"	要 + Verb
"Before" in general	以前 + Subj. + Verb + Obj.
"Even more" with "geng"	更 + Adj.
Expressing "with" with "gen"	跟…… + Verb
Change of state with "le"	……了
Expressing lateness with "cai"	才
Emphasizing quantity with "dou"	大家 / 很多人 + 都……
Expressing earliness with "jiu"	就

Expressing completion with "le"	Subj. + Verb + 了 + Obj.
Complements with "dao', "gei" and "zai"	V + 到 / 給 / 在 ……
Expressing duration with "le"	Verb + 了 + Duration
Sequencing past events with "houlai"	……，後來……
Using "ji" to mean "several"	Subj. + 在 + Place + Verb
CHAPTER 2	
After a specific time	Time/Time phrase + 以後
Two words for "but"	Statement, 可是/但是 + transitional statement
"Yinggai" for should	應該 / 該 + Verb
Adjectives with "name" and "zheme"	那麼 / 這麼 + Adj.
Yes-no questions with "ma"	……嗎?
Modifying nouns with phrase + "de"	(Phrase) + 的 + Noun
"Already" with "yijing"	已經……了
Aspect particle "zhe"	Verb+ 著
Expressing permission	可以 + Verb
Basic comparisons with "yiyang"	Noun 1 + 跟 + Noun 2 + 一樣 + Adj.
Before a specific time	Time / Verb+ 以前
Negative commands with "bie"	別 + Verb
CHAPTER 3	
Positive and negative potential complements	Verb + 得 / 不 ……
Expressing "a little too" with "you dian"	有點 (兒) + Adj.
Using "dui"	對 + Noun……
Using "zai" with verbs	Subj. + 在 + Place + Verb
Ordinal numbers with "di"	第 + Number (+ Measure Word)
"Just" with "gang"	Subj. + 剛 + Verb
Expressing "a bit too"	Adj.+（一）點兒

Verbing briefly	Verb + 一下
"Some" using "yixie"	一些 + Noun
Verbs with "gei"	Subj. + 給 + Target + Verb + Obj.
Expressing a learned skill	Subj. + 會 + Verb + Obj.
Simultaneous tasks with "yibian"	(一)邊 + Verb, (一)邊 + Verb
Suggestions with "ba"	……吧
Expressing location with "zai…shang/xia/li"	在 + Location + 上/下/裡/旁邊
"Shi… de" construction	是……的
Turning adjectives into adverbs	Adj. + 地 + Verb
Measure words for verbs	Verb + Number + Measure Word
"-wan" result complement	Subj. + Verb + 完 + Obj.
Verb reduplication with "yi"	Verb + 一 + Verb
Comparing "chao" "xiang" and "wang"	朝 vs 向 vs 往

CHAPTER 4

Expressing actions in progress	(正)在 + Verb
Reduplication of adjectives	Adj. + Adj.
Softening speech with "ba"	……吧。
"Not very" with "bu zenme"	不怎麼 + Adj.
Adding emphasis with "jiushi"	就是
Indicating a number in excess	Number + 多
Appearance with "kanqilai"	看起來……
Basic comparisons with "bi"	Noun 1 + 比 + Noun 2 + Adj.
Negative commands with "bu yao"	不要 + Verb
Direction complement	Verb (+ Direction) + 來 / 去
Questions with "le ma"	Verb + 了 + 嗎?
Result complement "-cuo"	Verb + 錯

CHAPTER 5

Expressing "excessively" with "tai"	太 + Adj. + 了

"De" (modal particle)	······ 的
Expressing "otherwise" with "yaobu"	要不······

CHAPTER 6

Verbs with "gei"	Subj. + 給 + Target + Verb + Obj.

CHAPTER 7

About to happen with "kuai… le"	快 + Verb/Verb Phrase + 了
Intensifying with "duo"	Subj. + 多 + Adj.

CHAPTER 8

"As long as" with "zhiyao"	只要······，就······
Expressing duration (ongoing)	Verb + 了 + Duration + 了
"Never again" with "zai ye bu"	再也不 + Verb

CHAPTER 9

Expressing purpose with "weile"	為了 + Purpose + Verb
Mistakenly think that	以為······
Expressing duration of inaction	Subj. + Duration + 沒 + Verb + Obj.+ 了

CHAPTER 10

Asking why with "zenme"	怎麼······?

CHAPTER 11

There are no new grammar points in this chapter.

CHAPTER 12

Softening the tone of questions with "ne"	······ 呢?

Other Stories from Mandarin Companion

Level 1 Readers: 300 Characters

The Sixty Year Dream 《六十年的夢》
based on Rip Van Winkle by Washington Irving

Zhou Xuefa (Rip Van Winkle) is well loved by everyone in his town, except his nagging wife. One day after a bad scolding from his wife, he goes for a walk into the mountains and meets a mysterious old man. After drinking some wine offered by the old man, Zhou Xuefa falls into a deep sleep. He awakes to a time very different from what he once knew.

The Monkey's Paw 《猴爪》
by W. W. Jacobs

Mr. and Mrs. Zhang live with their grown son. One day an old friend comes to visit and tells of a monkey's paw that has magical powers to grant three wishes to the holder. Against his better judgment, he reluctantly gives the monkey paw to the Zhang family, with a warning that the wishes come with a great price for trying to change fate.

The Country of the Blind 《盲人國》
by H. G. Wells

Chen Fangyuan finds himself trapped in a valley with a people for whom a disease has eliminated their vision and no longer have a concept of sight. His insistence that he can see causes the entire community to think he is crazy. Then one day the village doctors propose a disturbing cure for his insanity.

Sherlock Holmes and the Case of the Curly-Haired Company 《捲髮公司的案子》
based on The Red Headed League by Sir Arthur Conan Doyle

Mr. Xie was recently hired by the Curly Haired Company to copy articles from a book. He was selected from hundreds of applicants because of his very curly hair. When the company unexpectedly closes, Mr. Xie visits Gao Ming (Sherlock Holmes) with his strange story. Gao Ming is certain something is not right, but will he solve the mystery in time?

Level 2 Readers: 450 Characters

Great Expectations: Part 1 《美好的前途（上）》
by Charles Dickens

In Part 1, Xiaomao is raised by his short-tempered older sister and her husband outside of Shanghai. After meeting the beautiful Bingbing (Estella), Xiaomao dreams of leaving his life of poverty behind. His prospects for the future are bleak, until one day a mysterious benefactor gives Xiaomao the opportunity of a lifetime.

Great Expectations: Part 2 《美好的前途（下）》
by Charles Dickens

In Part 2, Xiaomao (Pip) leaves his life of poverty behind to seek his fortunes in Shanghai and win the heart of the beautiful yet cold-hearted Bingbing (Estella). Xiaomao's world is turned upside down when his mysterious benefactor is revealed and his deepest secrets are brought into the light of day.

Journey to the Center of the Earth 《地心遊記》
by Jules Verne

Join Professor Luo and his niece Xiaojing in their daring quest down the mouth of a volcano to reach the center of the earth. Guided by a mysterious passage on an ancient parchment and accompanied by their faithful guide Lao Xu, the three explorers encounter subterranean phenomena, prehistoric animals, and vast underground seas.

Mandarin Companion is producing a growing library of graded readers for Chinese language learners.

Visit our website for the newest books available:

www.MandarinCompanion.com

Lightning Source UK Ltd.
Milton Keynes UK
UKHW05f0331240718
326185UK00008B/54/P